CLEVELAND
BROWNS

RICHARD RAMBECK

CREATIVE C EDUCATION INC.

Published by Creative Education, Inc.
123 S. Broad Street, Mankato, Minnesota 56001

Designed by Rita Marshall

Cover illustration by Lance Hidy Associates

Photos by Allsport USA, Focus On Sports, Sportschrome,
Third Coast and Wide World Photos

Library of Congress Cataloging-in-Publication Data

Rambeck, Richard.
   Cleveland Browns/Richard Rambeck.
   p.   cm.
   ISBN 0-88682-363-3
   1. Cleveland Browns (Football team)—History.   I. Title.
GV956.C6R36   1990
796.332′64′0977132—dc20   90-41252
                                                     CIP

Cleveland, like many American towns, was named after a city in England. The Cleveland in the United States has grown to be the largest city in the state of Ohio. It is located in the northeastern corner of the state, on Lake Erie. Although Cleveland is not in the middle of Ohio, it is a major center of the state's economy. It has a busy port; ships carrying goods up the St. Lawrence Seaway dock on Cleveland's waterfront. Lake Erie dominates the view from just about any location in the city, and is responsible for many of Cleveland's weather patterns, as heavy winds often blow inland off the lake. The city also is known for bitterly cold winters. The winds and the cold cause some

An early Cleveland star, Dub Jones (#86).

people to refer to Cleveland as the "Mistake by the Lake." Cleveland a mistake? It certainly has been for visiting pro football teams trying to claim victories in the shadow of Lake Erie.

Since 1946, Cleveland has been home to a pro football team that has been, with rare exceptions, a consistent winner in the National Football League. The story of the Cleveland Browns is unique. Even the team nickname is unique. The Browns aren't named after the color brown; they are named after their first coach, Paul Brown, the man who built the team into a championship franchise.

As good as Brown was as a coach, he really didn't want the team named after him. But Brown told Cleveland owner Arthur (Mickey) McBride that he didn't want the team called the Panthers, either. The fans had chosen the name Panthers in a contest to name the team. Brown didn't like the name, because a pro football team in Cleveland during the 1920s had been called the Panthers. The Cleveland Panthers were losers, and Paul Brown didn't want his team associated with losers. So another contest was held to name the team. The winning choice was Browns, and this name stuck, despite the objections of the coach.

The first player signed by the Browns was tailback and future Hall of Famer Otto Graham.

OTTO IS AWESOME

The Cleveland Browns played their first season in 1946. However, they didn't play in the NFL; they were members of the brand-new All-American Football Conference. The Browns were not the only members of the AAFC, but they were the only champions in the four-year history of the league. After Cleveland's fourth consecutive championship in 1949, the AAFC's best teams were accepted

A Cleveland winner, linebacker Clay Matthews.

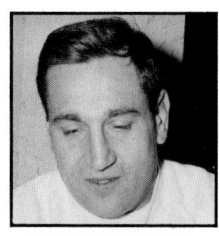

Place-kicker Lou Groza was one of seven Browns named to the Pro Bowl.

into the NFL. As good as the Browns had been in the AAFC, no one expected them to be one of the top teams in the NFL. "You're in a real league now," NFL people told the Browns.

But Paul Brown knew his team could play with anybody, mainly because the Browns had a quarterback who was as good as anyone in the game. Otto Graham began his pro football career as a rookie with the Browns in 1946. The rookie quarterback and the Browns grew into greatness together. But some people wondered just how good Graham was. Unlike other quarterbacks at that time, Graham didn't call the plays on the field. Paul Brown sent in messengers, usually offensive guards, with the calls. Even so, Graham said he had a lot to do with what plays the Browns ran.

"I believe the fellows playing pro ball are actually playing coaches," Graham said. "They know a lot better than anyone else what they can do at a given moment. There were times when I ignored Paul's calls. When my plays worked, he didn't say much. When they didn't, he let me know about it."

The first game the Browns ever played in the NFL was against the Philadelphia Eagles in 1950. Because the Eagles had won the NFL title in 1949, it was a matchup of the champions of the AAFC against the champions of the NFL. More than seventy thousand Eagles' fans jammed Philadelphia's Franklin Field to watch the Eagles and Browns battle. The Philadelphia fans expected their team to show Cleveland who the real champs were. But Graham, fullback Marion Motley, and receiver Dante Lavelli put on quite a show, and when it was all over, the "real" champs were the Browns. They defeated the Eagles 35-10.

The Browns' success continued throughout their first season in the NFL. They wound up winning the league title in 1950, the team's fifth straight championship but first in the NFL. Cleveland also made it to the championship game in 1951, but the Los Angeles Rams beat the Browns 24-17. For the first time in their history, the Browns weren't champions. "I let you down, Paul," Graham said to his coach after the loss to Los Angeles. "It's part of living," Brown replied. "Nothing to do now but forget it and start thinking of next season."

Quarterback Otto Graham passed for 2205 yards and seventeen touchdowns for the season.

Led by Graham, the Browns continued to claim division titles, winning in both 1952 and 1953. But they lost the NFL championship to Detroit both times. Despite those setbacks, the team remained confident, which it had every reason to be. No team had more offensive talent than the Browns. Graham had two great pass catchers, Dante Lavelli and Mac Speedie. The running game was led by Dub Jones and Marion Motley, a 240-pound fullback who was bigger than almost all of the linemen. And when the Browns couldn't get the ball in the end zone, they would call on legendary place-kicker Lou "The Toe" Groza to boot field goals.

But the key was Graham. The Browns believed that if he was on the field, the team could not be defeated. Against San Francisco in a 1953 game, Graham was sent to the sidelines by a vicious hit. Still groggy, he returned in the second half to complete nine of his last ten passes as Cleveland rallied to win 23-21.

At the beginning of the 1954 season, something strange happened to the Browns. They started the year by losing two of their first three games. For the first time in their nine-year history, the Browns were in danger of not

Wide receiver Webster Slaughter, (pages 10–11).

Marion Motley was the club's rushing leader, gaining 444 yards during the season.

playing in a championship game at the end of a season. But Graham pulled the team together, and Cleveland won all but one of its remaining games. For the fourth year in a row, the Browns were Eastern Division champions. For the third year in a row, the opponent in the NFL title game was the Detroit Lions, who had won the league championship in 1952 and 1953. This year, though, the Browns did not wind up second best.

Playing perhaps his finest game as a professional, Graham completed nine of twelve passes for 163 yards and three touchdowns. He scored three more times on runs. As the clock ticked down, Paul Brown took Graham out of the game. The eighty thousand fans in Cleveland's Municipal Stadium stood on their feet and roared for Graham. Behind the strength of his efforts Cleveland won 56-10.

In the locker room after the game, Graham announced he was retiring. "You've got to quit sometime, and it's great to quit while you're on top," he commented. But Paul Brown wasn't convinced that Graham was ready to hang up his cleats. "Otto has said nothing to me about it," Brown replied. "We'll see what happens next summer. Why should a guy who did what he did out there today retire?"

When training camp started before the 1955 season, Otto Graham was nowhere to be seen. The Browns apparently would have to play without him. Paul Brown tried to find a new quarterback, but no one in camp was anywhere near as good as Graham was. One day, Brown went back to his office and called Graham. "We need you," Brown urged. Graham agreed to return.

Led by the thirty-four-year-old Graham, the Browns rolled to another division title, their tenth in ten years. In the NFL title game, Graham led the Browns to a 38-14 victory over the Los Angeles Rams. "Graham is the greatest ever to play the quarterback position in pro football," an excited Brown said after the game. "He can throw, and he can run. More than that, he's a great inspiration for the rest of the team." A newspaper reporter asked Brown if he would try to get Graham to play again in 1956. "No," Brown answered. "I imposed on him once, and that's enough."

1 9 5 5

Veteran Otto Graham was a Pro Bowl selection for the fifth consecutive season.

What made Graham so good? "I was accurate," Graham said. "I was extremely accurate. A coach would tell me where to throw the ball and when to throw it. And I'd do it. It was a gift, a God-given gift." With Graham as quarterback, the Browns won seven league titles in ten years. No pro football team has ever been so good consistently for so long. After Graham retired, Cleveland fans wondered where the team would find its next superstar, and when it would find him. As it turned out, it took one year.

A GREAT BROWN, BESIDES PAUL, FOR THE BROWNS

In the 1957 draft, the Browns selected Syracuse University running back Jim Brown, who became a star in his rookie year. The six feet 228-pound Brown was not only one of the biggest running backs in the league, he was one of the strongest. Brown ran over tackler after tackler. "One thing that helps me is my running style," Brown said. "I don't go into the line in the traditional fullback manner. You don't find me leading with my head. Most of the time the contact is only my shoulder pads. Normally, I start with small steps so I'll be able to turn or slide toward the open-

Wide receiver Gary Collins led the league with thirteen touchdown receptions.

ing. When a tackler comes at me, I drop the shoulder. The runner's shoulder should be the first thing to hit the tackler."

The Browns knew they had a weapon in Brown. He was almost indestructible, but some fans wondered if the Browns were using their star fullback too much. After one game, a reporter asked Jim Brown if he was getting too much work. After all, the reporter commented, Brown had carried the ball thirty-four times in the game. Brown looked the reporter squarely in the eye and said, "If he [Paul Brown] says carry fifty times, then I carry fifty times."

Paul Brown wasn't about to force Jim Brown to carry that many times, but the Cleveland coach knew he could afford to use his durable star running back a lot. "When you have a big gun, you shoot it," Paul Brown said. "I remember a time when Jim smashed into a tackler and got up and walked back to the huddle. The tackler got up and followed Jim into our huddle, like a boxer staggering to the wrong corner. His teammates had to get him. Maybe the people who have been trying to stop Jim are taking the beating."

But unlike Otto Graham, Jim Brown didn't have much luck leading the Cleveland Browns to a championship. He was the NFL's leading rusher almost every year, but the Browns never found themselves at the top. In 1962 new Browns' owner Art Modell fired Paul Brown. Paul Brown and Jim Brown hadn't gotten along. New coach Blanton Collier worked to develop a good relationship with Brown. His efforts paid off.

The Browns were talking about winning a championship in 1964. In addition to Jim Brown's running game,

Like Brown, Ernest Byner was a strong runner.

Jim Brown led the league in rushing yardage for the second consecutive season.

Cleveland had developed a fine passing attack. Quarterback Frank Ryan had two excellent receivers, sure-handed Gary Collins and speedy Paul Warfield, whose smooth stride resembled that of an antelope. The defense was built around Doug Atkins, an end who would be elected to the pro football Hall of Fame.

The Browns spent most of the 1964 season in first place, but a late-season loss to the St. Louis Cardinals damaged Cleveland's title hopes. The Browns regrouped, however, and won their final game of the regular season 52-20 over the New York Giants. That victory enabled Cleveland to finish just ahead of the Cardinals in the Eastern Division. Brown had once again run wild, to move Cleveland into the playoffs.

"The thing that stands out unforgettably in my mind is his attitude," said Cleveland assistant coach Dub Jones of Brown. "After we lost to the Cardinals, he showed me he was a man. Usually, when the walls start crumbling, the weaker men crumble with them. He helped mend the walls. He did a great job of attitude rebuilding."

Jim Brown and Cleveland weren't through. They faced the Baltimore Colts in the championship game at Cleveland. The game was scoreless at halftime, but the Browns came out in the second half determined to claim their first league title since 1955. Brown gained 114 yards on twenty-seven carries, with most of those yards coming in the second half. Frank Ryan connected with Gary Collins on a couple of scoring passes. Behind these fine contributions the Browns rolled to a 27-0 victory.

Afterwards, reporters asked Jim Brown what the turning point of the game was. "When we held them scoreless in the first half," Brown said. "We proved to ourselves they were human, not supermen. There was pleasure in knowing we could give them a hard time, fight them toe-to-toe."

As Brown took off his football gear, head coach Blanton Collier came over and greeted his star. "I tried to get over before, Jim, but there were too many people coming at me," Collier remarked. "I want to thank you for your leadership."

Later that day, Brown walked into the Browns' victory party. Everyone stood and applauded the man who was considered the best running back ever to play pro football. When the cheering finally died down, one player said, "That applause wasn't for his great playing. It was to let him know how much we think of him as a person."

After the 1965 season, Brown shocked the football world by retiring. He was only thirty years old and had several good years left in him. But Brown said the football part of his life was over. Jim Brown left the game as the NFL's all-time leading rusher. It would take twenty years before another running back, Chicago's Walter Payton, would break Brown's yardage record.

After Brown retired, Cleveland still kept winning, thanks to running back Leroy Kelly and quarterbacks Frank Ryan and Bill Nelson. In 1970 when the American Football League and National Football League merged, the Browns were moved to the Central Division of the American Football Conference. Other teams in the division included Pittsburgh, Houston, and the Browns' archrivals, the Cincinnati Bengals. During the early 1970s, both Pittsburgh and Cincinnati built powerful teams. The Browns, meanwhile, slumped to third in the division. Owner Art Modell wasn't used to this. He needed to find someone to restore the winning ways to the Cleveland franchise.

1 9 6 8

Running back Leroy Kelly rushed for sixteen touchdowns —tops in the league.

Cleveland still eyes a Super Bowl victory, (pages 18–19).

Sam Rutigliano guided the Browns to an 8-8 record in his first season as head coach.

In 1978, Modell hired Sam Rutigliano to replace Forrest Gregg as head coach. Rutigliano built his team around a quarterback who wasn't very tall and who didn't have a very strong arm. "There are high school quarterbacks with stronger arms than mine," said Brian Sipe, Rutigliano's choice to lead the Browns. The Cleveland coach knew Sipe didn't have a great arm, but Rutigliano saw something special in Sipe's attitude. "Brian had been supercompetitive since he was a little kid," Rutigliano said. "I loved it. Don Coryell, who coached Brian in college, told me, 'He'll battle for you.' Brian was the most competitive football player, regardless of position, I had ever known. He was intelligent, creative, and tough, and he was at his best in crucial situations. We were destined to have many last-minute wins engineered by Brian. When he came to the sideline during those timeouts close to the end of the games, he always gave me that feeling of utmost confidence. The tighter the circumstances, the more leadership he showed."

Sipe struggled at times during the 1978 season. Some of the Cleveland fans began booing him and demanding another quarterback. But Rutigliano stayed with Sipe. After one game that season, Sipe came to Rutigliano's office. "Coach," Sipe said, "the most important thing for us to do is to win. I'm your quarterback. I'm the guy you can win with now and in the future."

Rutigliano remembered this scene. "I looked at Brian," the Cleveland coach remembered. "He wasn't being cocky. He was simply confident. I said, 'Brian, we made our commitment to you, and that's that. You're our quarterback.'"

Eventually, Sipe and the Browns started to get better. They went 8-8 in 1978 and 9-7 in 1979, just missing the playoffs. In 1979 the Browns won seven games with fourth-quarter heroics. The team became known as the "Kardiac Kids" because of its heart-stopping finishes. Sipe, wide receivers Reggie Rucker and Ricky Feacher, and tight end Ozzie Newsome produced some incredible fourth-quarter comebacks. In addition, running backs Mike Pruitt and Greg Pruitt (no relation) provided a balanced attack.

The Browns' leader, quarterback Brian Sipe, was named the NFL's Most Valuable Player.

The Kardiac Kids became the darlings of the news media. Len Dawson, a former great quarterback with the Kansas City Chiefs, was doing a story on the Browns and Sipe for NBC-TV during the 1979 season. "I talked to the Cleveland players," Dawson said, "and they really believe he [Sipe] can get it done. The receivers feel he'll get them the ball if they get open." Paul Zimmerman, a pro football writer for *Sports Illustrated,* called Sipe "the ultimate two-minute quarterback" because of the many late-game drives that he was able to produce.

In 1980 Sipe and the Browns put it all together. They won the AFC Central Division title and secured home-field advantage throughout the AFC playoffs. Any team trying to prevent the Browns from getting into the Super Bowl would have to win in cold, windy Cleveland Municipal Stadium. The Oakland Raiders came to Cleveland hoping to do just that.

Late in the game, the Raiders had a 14-12 lead, but Sipe

Explosive running talent Eric Metcalf.

was in the middle of a potential game-winning drive. Deep in Raider territory, Sipe went back to pass, looking for a receiver in the end zone. He scrambled around, nearly fell, and then threw for the touchdown. But when the ball came down, it was in the hands of Oakland's Mike Davis. After the interception, Rutigliano put his arms around Sipe and said, "Brian, I love you. You had a great year. I know how tough this is for you, but you gotta put it behind you." Oakland won 14-12 and went on to claim a Super Bowl title.

1 9 8 4

Tight end Ozzie Newsome caught eighty-nine passes for the second straight season.

Unfortunately, the Kardiac Kids had reached their peak. The outcome of the 1980 playoffs haunted the team. After the 1983 season, Sipe jumped to the new United States Football League. Rutigliano was fired after the 1984 season. The new coach was Marty Schottenheimer. And the new quarterback was a young star who had grown up near Cleveland. Bernie Kosar went to the University of Miami in Florida, but when he graduated, Kosar said he wanted to play for one team and only one team—the Cleveland Browns.

KOSAR ZEROS IN ON CLEVELAND

Kosar got his wish when the Browns picked him in the 1985 NFL Supplemental Draft, which is held a few weeks after the regular draft. Kosar, who took only three years to finish college, graduated from Miami after the regular draft but in time to put his name in the supplemental draft. When he arrived at the Browns' training camp, Kosar immediately impressed his teammates with his intelligence and leadership abilities. He became a starter right away.

23

24   *Clockwise: Bernie Kosar, Kevin Mack, Ernest Byner, Frank Minnifield.*

"I don't understand it, but he can focus on everything and not overload," said Browns' backup quarterback Gary Danielson. "I'm not talking about blocking schemes and coverages. I mean things like how many people are in the stands, how many timeouts are left, where the stadium speakers are, why we have Gatorade and not Coke. He'll not only know who the officials are, he'll know where they are from. . . . He'll take all this stuff and use it to find an angle, something to help him win."

Kosar combines intelligence with a deadly accuracy. "He knows the game," said Phoenix Cardinals' guard Joe Bostic. "He knows what's going on. He says, 'Ball, go here.'" But what amazes people about Kosar isn't his ability to throw the ball wherever he wants to throw it; it's the *way* he throws the ball that's unique. "He throws sidearm, underhand, submarine, spitball, slider, knuckleball, and that's only in our first possession," joked owner Art Modell. "But you know what? He gets it there."

Kosar admits his throwing style is a bit odd. "I have practiced trying to throw overhand," he said. "But when it gets down to it, I always go back to what I'm comfortable with. I've probably thrown as many passes underhand in this league as I have straight overhand. . . . When I throw, I'll pick out a part of the receiver's body to throw to. Very rarely will I aim for the chest. For two reasons. One, if the ball is high, it can be deflected. And two, you don't see guys extremely wide open in this league."

Kosar and the Browns became the top team in the AFC's Central Division. The offense was effective in the air, thanks to Kosar and receivers Webster Slaughter, Brian Brennan, and Ozzie Newsome, and on the ground, with running backs Kevin Mack and Ernest Byner carrying the

1 9 8 5

Browns' running back Ernest Byner rushed for over 1000 yards during the season.

Clay Matthews (#57).

Cleveland's fine record of 12-4 brought to mind the championship teams of the 1960s, led by Jim Brown (right).

load. On defense cornerbacks Frank Minnifield and Hanford Dixon were both Pro Bowl selections, but veteran linebacker Clay Matthews might have been Cleveland's best all-around defender.

Behind these stars in 1986, Cleveland posted the best record in the AFC, 12-4. But in their first playoff game, the Browns fell behind the upset-minded New York Jets. Late in the contest, New York's Mark Gastineau was called for roughing the passer when he crashed into Kosar well after the Cleveland quarterback released the ball. Kosar got up and was more determined than ever to rally the Browns. "I saw a look in his eyes I'd never seen before," remembered Ozzie Newsome. "He was not going to be denied. He was going to find a way to win that football game."

And Kosar did find a way. With the Browns trailing 20-10, Kosar engineered two long drives. The first one produced a touchdown and the second a game-tying field goal. The Browns wound up winning 23-20 in overtime.

The following week in Cleveland, Kosar and the Browns needed to beat the Denver Broncos to earn a spot in the Super Bowl. Late in the fourth quarter, Kosar hit Brian Brennan on a long touchdown pass, and the Browns led 20-13. But the Broncos, behind quarterback John Elway, drove to a tying touchdown with less than a minute left. Denver won the game in overtime with a field goal, 23-20, disappointing more than eighty thousand fans in Cleveland Municipal Stadium.

The Browns claimed the Central Division title again in 1987 and advanced to the AFC title game to meet, once again, the Denver Broncos. This time, the game was in Denver. And this time, it was the Broncos who took the early lead. Denver built its advantage to 31-10 in the third quarter, but then Kosar went to work. Cleveland scored three touchdowns to tie the game 31-31. Elway rebounded and led the Broncos on a scoring drive to make the score 38-31. But the Browns didn't quit. "There are no quitters on this team," Kosar said after the game. Kosar moved the Browns to the shadow of Denver's goal line, but a fumble ended Cleveland's dreams of a Super Bowl.

Even though the Browns lost, people couldn't stop talking about how good Kosar had been. Kosar was a star, and everybody knew it. But Bernie just wanted to be one of the guys. "That's what he is, a normal kid from anybody's neighborhood," remarked Cleveland tackle Paul Farren. But this kid had exceptional ability, and there was no denying how much he meant to the Browns. "I'd rather blend ·in," Kosar said. "It's impossible because I'm the quarterback, I know. But I'd like to."

1 9 8 8

Quarterback Bernie Kosar's fine performance led many critics to call him one of the NFL's finest signal-callers.

The lightning fast Webster Slaughter.

All-Pro tackle Michael Dean Perry. 31

*Wide receiver
Webster Slaughter
was club leader in
receptions and pass
receiving yardage.*

Led by Kosar, the Browns have become one of the top teams in the AFC. A new coach, Bud Carson, nearly led Cleveland to the Super Bowl in 1989, his first year as the Browns' head man. For the third time in four years, Cleveland met Denver in the conference title game. Unfortunately, for the third time in four years, the Broncos beat the Browns and advanced to the Super Bowl.

But Cleveland's future is bright. Kosar is only in his mid-twenties. The Browns' two outstanding wide receivers, Webster Slaughter and Reggie Langhorne, are also young. The team has added a quick, explosive running back in Eric Metcalf, an ideal complement to Kevin Mack and his power runs. Ozzie Newsome, who caught more passes than any tight end in the history of the NFL, had announced his retirement after the 1989 season, but then he changed his mind. Lawyer Tillman, an outstanding talent at wide receiver, may be molded to eventually replace Newsome.

The defense is solid, and it figures to get better because Bud Carson made his reputation in the NFL as a defensive coordinator for several teams. Cornerback Frank Minnifield and linebacker Clay Matthews continue have few peers at their positions. Defensive lineman Michael Dean Perry, brother of William "The Refrigerator" Perry of the Chicago Bears, is one of the best young pass rushers in pro football.

The Browns' young stars are on a mission. Amazingly, Cleveland has never played in a Super Bowl. This is the franchise that competed in ten consecutive league championship games from 1946 to 1955. The current Browns desperately want to taste some of that success. Thanks to a solid foundation of talent, the Browns appear ready for Super things in the nineties.